760
SHE

D0119549

Directions In Art
Printmaking

Louisa Sherman & Dianne Hofmeyr

Heinemann
LIBRARY

www.heinemann.co.uk/library

Visit our website to find out more information about Heinemann Library books.

To order:

☎ Phone 44 (0) 1865 888066

🖹 Send a fax to 44 (0) 1865 314091

💻 Visit the Heinemann Bookshop at www.heinemann.co.uk/library to browse our catalogue and order online.

First published in Great Britain by Heinemann Library, Halley Court, Jordan Hill, Oxford OX2 8EJ, part of Harcourt Education. Heinemann is a registered trademark of Harcourt Education Ltd.

Editorial: Lucy Thunder and Helen Cannons
Design: Jo Hinton-Malivoire and AMR
Picture Research: Hannah Taylor and Elaine Willis
Production: Edward Moore

Originated by Ambassador Litho Ltd
Printed and bound in China by South China Printing Company

ISBN 0 431 17645 0
07 06 05 04 03
10 9 8 7 6 5 4 3 2 1

British Library Cataloguing in Publication Data
Hofmeyr, Dianne and Sherman, Louisa
Printmaking. – (Directions in art)
769.9
A full catalogue record for this book is available from the British Library.

Acknowledgements
The Publishers would like to thank the following for permission to reproduce photographs: Art Resource / The Andy Warhol Foundation for the Visual Arts / ARS, NY and DACS p. **41**; Vija Celmins / McKee Gallery pp. **13, 14**; Corbis / George H Huey p. **4**; Alan Cristea Gallery / Richard Hamilton 2003. All rights reserved, DACS p. **21**; Peter Diog / Tate London 2003 pp. **17, 18**; Durst p. **34**; William Kentridge pp. 25, 27; David Krut Fine Art Inc. p. **26**; The Estate of Roy Lichtenstein / DACS 2003 pp. **29t, 30**; Andrew Mummery Gallery pp. **9, 11**; National Gallery of Art, Washington p. **15**; Niedersachsische Landesmuseum, Hanover, Germany / Bridgeman Art Library / The Andy Warhol Foundation for the Visual Arts / ARS, NY and DACS 2003 p. **42**; Julian Opie / Alan Cristea Gallery pp. **33, 35**; Paula Rego / Courtesy of Marlborough Fine Art, London pp. **37, 39**; Tate London 2003 / Richard Hamilton 2003. All Rights Reserved, DACS p. **23**; Kim Westcott p. **45**; Adrian Wiszniewski / Glasgow Print Studio p. **47**, / The Paragon Press pp. **48, 49**.

Cover photograph of *Portrait of Dieter Roth* (1998) by Richard Hamilton reproduced with permission of Alan Cristea Gallery / Richard Hamilton 2003. All rights reserved DACS.

The publishers would like to thank Richard Stemp, Gallery Educator at the Tate, London, for his assistance in the preparation of this book

CONTENTS

Any words appearing in the text in bold, **like this**, are explained in the Glossary.

WHAT IS PRINTMAKING?

We can all remember the pleasure of making footprints in the sand or drawing in soil with a stick. These kinds of basic images were also made by early cave dwellers whose handprints on rock faces were the first, direct prints. Since early times handprints were made as either positive or negative images. Positive prints were the most common and the hand was covered in paint and then printed directly on to the rock face. Negative handprints, as you can see in the picture below, were made by using the hand as a stencil and spraying around it with paint. The same imagination behind those first prints prompted a rich tradition of prints and printmaking that followed down the centuries.

Today, we think of a print as a work of art printed in ink on paper of which there are multiple copies. Prints are art works created not by drawing directly on to paper, but by an indirect method. The image is made on to a surface such as wood, metal or stone and then transferred to paper. In this way, multiple copies of the work can be made.

These handprints, from the famous Painted Cave at the Anasazi ruins in Arizona, USA, are an early example of printmaking. They were made around AD 450 to AD 1300.

Traditional methods of printmaking

In traditional printmaking, artists work directly on to their chosen surface to produce an image, often with the help of master printers who are trained specifically to produce prints. There are several different ways to do this. Artists using **relief printing** techniques such as **woodcut** or wood engraving will cut an image directly into the woodblock.

In **intaglio** techniques, such as drypoint (see pages 26–27), **etching** (see page 38) and aquatint (see page 18), artists press ink into lines etched or engraved into the surface of a **plate**. In **lithography**, the artist draws directly with a greasy crayon on to a flat limestone slab before it is treated for printing. In **screenprint** artists prepare their own stencils for printing. These methods were commonly used in the 19th and early 20th centuries, but later new technologies such as photography and **digital printing** have brought about far-reaching changes in printmaking.

Lithography

Lithography is a printmaking technique in which the image is drawn on to a flat slab of limestone or a specially prepared metal plate. Drawings can be made with greasy pencils, crayons or lithographic ink, also called *tusche*. The plate or stone is then treated to retain water in the areas not drawn on. When the stone or plate is rolled up with printing ink, the greasy drawing picks up the ink. The rest of the stone or plate retains water and will repel ink. A sheet of paper is placed on to the inked plate or stone and is then passed through a lithographic press. The image transfers from the stone or metal surface, to the paper.

Picasso's Le Picador II *(1961) is a lithographic print.*

20th century prints and photography

Important artists like Pablo Picasso (1881–1973), Henri Matisse (1869–1954) and Emile Nolde (1867–1956) turned increasingly to printmaking in the 20th century. Gradually, printmaking became a major form of artistic expression, taking its place alongside painting, drawing and sculpture.

Fine art printmaking also thrived as a result of the invention of photography in 1839. Before then, printmaking had been used to produce all kinds of everyday material, such as advertisements. Photography meant that mechanical printing processes were increasingly used to produce such work, freeing printmaking by hand to develop as an art form in its own right. Photography also played an important role in printmaking in other respects. Photographs became a source for images within printmaking, and photographic techniques were used to transfer images from film to screen or plate.

Many artists including Richard Hamilton (pages 20–23) and Andy Warhol (pages 40–43) produced some of their most significant works of art on paper using photographic techniques. The use of photography in printmaking caused a stir. It was thought by some to undermine the idea of the 'original' print.

The 'original' print

In traditional printmaking, the artist is directly involved in the creation of the print. Artists and printers aim to produce prints that are identical and they number the **editions**. If **print-runs** are too big, there is the danger of losing print quality. Also, too many copies of a print could reduce its value. It is therefore in the interests of artist and art dealers to control the production of 'original prints'. However, over recent years the idea of the 'original' print has been challenged by new ideas and technologies. Artists searching for new ways to express themselves have broadened the idea of printmaking beyond just handmade images. Another breakthrough that challenged what is considered 'original' was the first computer-generated prints made in London in the 1960s.

A new freedom in printmaking

The recent use of digital printing has, similar to photography before it, created new opportunities and challenges for the printmaking world. Traditionally, a print-run is limited to how long the **plate** or screen will last until it becomes worn and the image deteriorates. However digital printing can result in print-runs of thousands. Furthermore, new inks and papers with increased permanence have been specially developed and compare well with traditional papers and inks.

In digital printing, images may be recorded by camera and loaded on to computers for further manipulation before printing on paper or other materials. Digital printmaking has opened up exciting new possibilities for artists to explore in terms of technique. For example, Hamilton transfers his thorough understanding of photographic printmaking techniques to his digital printmaking, while Chila Kumari Burman (pages 8–11) and Julian Opie (pages 32–35) use digital images in their **installations** to create multiple prints for wallpaper and to compose murals and even car bumper stickers!

While many contemporary artists explore new digital technologies, others, like Kim Westcott (pages 44–45) and William Kentridge (pages 24–27), use old techniques in a new way. Westcott revives a traditional wax painting technique for her printmaking and Kentridge creates etchings, linocuts and **photogravure** prints that could almost be seen as 'stills' from his animated films. Others, such as Warhol and Hamilton, explored **conceptual** art issues in printmaking – where the idea behind the work is all-important. By doing this they brought printmaking, in the 1960s, into line with sculpture and painting. They also took up the French **Dada** and **Surrealist** artist Marcel Duchamp's (1887–1968) earlier idea that art is a 'choice of mind, not the cleverness of hand'. Duchamp exhibited a 'ready made' porcelain urinal entitled *Fountain* (1917), to illustrate that a work of art is determined by the artist's 'choice of mind' rather than the practical skills of painting, sculpture or printmaking.

Although the 'hand' of the artist or master printer still has to ink the plate, or click the computer key, it is exciting to see how printmaking contributes in a significant and varied way to today's art.

CHILA KUMARI BURMAN

Chila Kumari Burman is an artist whose works span printmaking, painting, drawing, mixed **media**, photography, video and film. She was born in 1957 in Liverpool, UK, and grew up near the seaside in Formby. At home the family spoke Punjabi, but Burman attended English schools in Liverpool before doing a Foundation Course at the Southport College of Art. She also attended the Slade School of Fine Art in London where she graduated in Fine Art in Printmaking in 1982. Burman has taught at different art schools across Britain. She has exhibited her work in Britain and in India, Canada, USA, Pakistan, Cuba and Africa. She lives and works in Haringey, London.

Influences from home and beyond

Burman's art reflects her own life very closely, dealing with her identity as an Asian woman. She explores the stereotype of Asian women being 'meek, mild and passive', as well as her own family history. **Dada**, **Surrealism**, Bollywood, Hindu philosophy, film, music, popular culture and her mother have all influenced her. Burman's heartfelt piece *Dad on a ship coming to Britain in the 50's and the three Queens* (1995) features her mother. The work shows three queens – her mother, her grandmother and the portrait of the Queen of England on a banknote. All three women are represented as queens in recognition of their endurance and achievements. By combining these pictures Burman cleverly shows us that she moves between two different cultures – her own Indian background and her life in Britain.

> *My recent work is concerned with autobiography, representation of the self, I have dealt with themes around history, dual cultural heritage, mythology, memory and photography, wild women...*
> CHILA KUMARI BURMAN

Working method

Burman uses a range of media including painting, photography and **digital printmaking** to suit the **installation** or display of her works in exhibition spaces. She often combines different techniques and unusual media such as **laser prints** and car spray paint. She also uses 'found' images and personal photographs that she reworks to explore the themes in her work. For example, in *Hello Girls* (1999) Burman, exhibited rows and rows of prints to form one large work.

Hello Girls is a reflection on the successful 1990s Wonderbra® advertisements, 'Hello Boys', which featured an alluring, 'sexy' image of a woman in a bra. In *Hello Girls*, Burman deals with western stereotypes and the portrayal of the Asian female, including taboos such as bras and breasts in Asian culture. Her work questions the attitudes towards women in these advertisements, in particular Asian and African women.

For-tune

In *For-tune* (2002; **Cibachrome**/Ilfochrome classic print on plastic paper), Burman further explores the coloured, patterned bras used in *Hello Girls*. Here she elaborates upon the idea of bras, but adds colourful flowers and *bindis* that she blends into an exotic, sumptuous array of colours, patterns and textures.

Ideals of beauty

Burman includes elements in *For-tune* such as the *bindi* and flowers that remind us of Hindu temples. The *bindi* is a traditional Hindu decoration applied to the forehead that marks the third eye, the home of conscious and sub-conscious awareness and thought in Hindu culture. Although the *bindi* has become a popular body decoration worldwide, Burman subtly questions whether we understand the significance of the *bindi* in Hindu culture. She does this in a playful and colourful manner, even though her concerns are serious. In *For-tune*, the artist protests against the modern preoccupation with glamour and beauty; she claims freedom for women to do with their bodies what they want and not to become slaves to the fashion industry.

We can look with pleasure at *For-tune's* beautiful colours and shapes, but Burman also reminds us that we should appreciate the female body with thoughtfulness, even the bodies of those we do not know well. She presents the viewer with a Hindu visual ideal of beauty, in contrast to Western ideals of beauty, desire and identity that dominate the **mass media**.

Technique

Burman uses a collage technique in *For-tune* to piece together this bright **composition**. She collected objects including animal prints and brightly coloured bras that represent Western fashion and beauty, and flowers and *bindis* that recall Hindu culture. She then arranged them in eight different compositions on a colour laser printer. After making the colour prints, she worked on the copies and re-photographed the completed eight images that were then printed to make up a larger Cibachrome.

A Cibachrome or C-Print is a high quality photographic printing process on to plastic paper. Images are printed from slides or transparencies on to paper that contains special dyes built into the paper rather than on the surface as in conventional colour prints. The process is known for its stable, fade-resistant brilliance and intense, sharp colours.

Girl art across cultures

In many ways Burman has been a groundbreaking artist in Britain who has become actively involved in issues of identity, class and gender. The 1980s, when Burman started practising her art, was a significant time in the British art world for many African, Asian and Caribbean artists.

There were many debates about race, identity and the role of art. These discussions helped to give a voice and identity to people from varied cultural backgrounds. Burman explores the issues of being a British–Asian. She also incorporates elements of other people's experiences of crossing from one culture into another.

In a work entitled *Automatic Rap: Don't Get Me Started* (1994), Burman explores how identities become merged by combining elements from punk, *bhangra* (Punjab folk music), reggae, rap, hip-hop, Hindi films, pop star imagery, graffiti and her own adolescence. This self-portrait has a rap text written over it: 'Wish I could go to discos, parties, dances, and have girlfriends and boyfriends like all the english girls and posh asian girls … hibernate to liberate – Don't get me started … let's Laugh and Dance … STRUGGLE, FIGHT, SHOUT, IZZAT/ RESPECT US NOW'.

In *Blue Apsaras* (1999), Burman explores the beauty of apsaras who are ancient Vedic Indian water and forest spirits. This work explores the cultural restrictions Asian women face in terms of dress. They are constantly torn between Western and Asian ways of behaviour.

Blue Apsaras *(1999) was created from collaged colour photocopies that were then photographed and printed as Cibachrome prints.*

VIJA CELMINS

Vija Celmins is a well known American painter, object-maker and **draughtswoman**. She is also a skilled printmaker using a wide range of processes in her art including wood **engraving**, **mezzotint** and stone **lithography**.

Celmins was born in Riga, the capital of Latvia, Eastern Europe, in 1938. During her childhood, the Celmins family escaped from war-torn Europe and eventually settled in Indianapolis, USA. Celmins graduated in 1962 with a degree in Fine Arts then moved to Los Angeles where she completed a Masters in Fine Arts from the University of California. She then joined their teaching staff. Celmins has since moved to New York where she lives and works. She has exhibited widely both in the USA and Europe.

Influences

While still at school and before she could speak any English, Celmins used to draw and paint. Some years later she spent a summer at Yale University where she came into contact with a group of artists and students, who influenced her to become a painter. Since the 1960s Celmins has used photographs as inspiration. A single photograph may serve as the basis for several different works of art.

Approach

Celmin's early **still-lives** are painted in an almost monochromatic, or single colour, palette of soft greys and whites. They reveal a sense of sadness and desolation that could be traced to her memories of violence and homelessness during her early childhood. From 1966 her focus shifted away from painting and she concentrated on detailed graphite pencil drawings of the sea, the desert and night skies.

Celmins has a fascination with space. After studying black and white photographs from expeditions to the moon in the 1960s, she realized that the layers of stars in the sky created distance. She believed that putting layers in drawings can prompt the viewer's thought processes and create a depth in the relationship between the viewer and the art object.

Celmin's printmaking extends over more than 35 **editions** made during the last 30 years. Of these, the *Sky*, *Ocean*, *Desert* and *Galaxy* prints are probably the most important as they represent the central themes in her work (see pages 14–15).

Celmins has been interested in the subject of spiders for several years. In *Web #2: Mezzotint* (2000), she portrays the delicate strands of the spider web in her usual grey shades. The mezzotint technique is ideal to achieve the continuous graded tones in this subtle image. The idea of layering also occurs in the spider's web. While looking at the finely drawn detail and observing the whole **composition** with its shifts of light and darkness, the viewer becomes trapped.

Web #2: Mezzotint *(2000). The fragile nature of a spider's web, that is both a nest and a trap, seems a reflection on the artist's traumatic childhood and loss of her home during World War II.*

Mezzotint

Mezzotint is a time-consuming printing process. First a tool with a serrated edge is used to roughen the **plate** all over, creating ridges called burrs. The design is made by polishing the plate smooth in some places and scraping to flatten the burrs in others. Some areas may be left with just the rough burrs exposed. The plate is then covered in ink, which is retained by all the rough parts. This creates a strong black when printed. The smoother parts hold less ink and so print a lighter tone. In this way a range of different tones are used to make up the image. The term mezzotint comes from the Italian *mezzo* meaning half and *tinto* meaning tint.

Ocean Surfaces 2000

Ocean Surfaces 2000 (2000), a wood engraving, is an interpretation of a photograph taken at Venice Beach, California. The finished engraving can easily be mistaken for a photograph as it has been cut in such a precise, realistic and detailed manner. Celmins has captured the movement and play of light upon the water without the images having an end or a beginning. There is no indication of scale. The distance between the viewer and the water constantly shifts between a close-up view looking at the detail of small water ripples and a longer shot moving into the distance as one's eye glances across the water.

Technique

Wood engraving is a **relief** printing technique where the image is printed from a raised surface. The design is cut with a knife or gouge from the **end grain** of a wood block. The wood grain of end grain blocks has no single direction, so the block can be cut freely in any direction to produce fine and intricate detail.

The density and layering effects in *Ocean Surfaces 2000* are achieved through the sharp contrast of white lines against a black field. The hardness of the wood Celmins has used allows her to work in tiny detail to capture the liquid, grey texture of the water's surface.

Vija Celmins (left) signing an edition of completed prints at the Gemini G.E.L. print workshop in Los Angeles, USA.

At home in nature

Celmins sharply observes the natural world, whether it is starry night skies, the rhythmic swell of the ocean, sand grains in the desert or the fragile silky threads of spider webs. Although her works look simple, they draw in viewers as the visual layers in her pictures unfold.

... aside from art, nature is one of the most amazing and comforting things to me. VIJA CELMINS

PETER DOIG

Peter Doig is a printmaker and painter who is famous for his atmospheric landscapes. He was born in Edinburgh, Scotland, in 1959, but his parents soon moved to Trinidad for a short time before settling in Canada. In 1979, Doig returned to Britain and, after completing his Foundation studies at the Wimbledon School of Art, he enrolled at St Martin's School of Art in 1980. Doig returned to his studies after time spent painting theatre scenery and in 1990 completed a Master of Arts degree at the Chelsea School of Art. Since then he has won many awards, but the Whitechapel Art Gallery's 'Whitechapel Artist Award' of 1991 gained him his first public recognition. Doig has participated in many group and solo exhibitions in Britain, Europe and North America.

Influences

Doig has been described as a Scottish–Canadian–English artist. His work really reflects two cultures – his themes speak of North America while the treatment of his images shows influences of his training in London.

Doig's works are obviously nostalgic and can easily be labelled as **kitsch**. However, looking deeper into his work, it becomes apparent that Doig deliberately uses both popular **mass media** reproductions and fine art references as his source material. He does not avoid the secret attraction we all share for 'chocolate box' sunsets and picturesque landscapes. Doig embraces these images and, together with experiences, emotions and photographs of his own childhood in North America, he presents us with 'sample' landscapes that refer to these stereotype landscapes.

Doig has been influenced by his childhood experiences of the Canadian landscape. His art has also taken on a broad range of subjects while exploring the theme of people's relationship with their environment. The artist captures 'versions' of landscapes, almost as if they are variations of existing landscape we are all familiar with. He uses a loose, pictorial technique rather similar to **Post-Impressionists** such as Pierre Bonnard, whose **figurative** works include flat **abstract** areas of paint. Doig's work shares similarities with the contemporary German photographer Andreas Gursky (b. 1955) who portrays modern leisure activities.

I often paint scenes with snow because snow somehow has this effect of drawing you inwards and is frequently used to suggest introspection and nostalgia and make-believe. PETER DOIG

Echoes of unease

Many of Doig's landscapes reflect upon places or events he has seen, knows well or imagines. As much as he is influenced by nature, he also responds to pop music, photography, video and the cinema. The climax in the closing scene from the 1980 film *Friday the 13th*, a mystery horror thriller, forms the basis of Doig's 1998 painting and subsequent print series entitled, *Echo Lake*. In the print *Echo Lake* (2000) Doig portrays a sketchily drawn policeman who stands at the water's edge looking as if something horrifying has just disappeared into the stormy water.

Echo Lake *(2000). Aquatint on paper. In this print, the stillness of the painted lake is replaced by choppy water and dark creepy shadows snaking across the surface.*

[no title] from the Ten Etchings series

Doig shows a preoccupation with the landscape that reveals both his own memories of his Canadian childhood as well as the Canadian peoples' attachment to the land. His own leisure interests are also connected to the outdoors and in the series *Ten Etchings* (1996) various snow scenes are featured. This series, Doig's first venture into printmaking, seems restrained. This could be due to the black and white colouring of the prints. Included in the series is the work *[no title]*. Here the artist skilfully uses both aquatint (see page 19) and **etching** techniques to suggest the mountain landscape. The whiteness of the paper in the etching is sharply highlighted by a trail of black skiers zigzagging across the surface.

Doig does not attempt to hide the emptiness of the landscape, but has ensured an interesting balance between black aquatinted shapes and blank background across the whole **composition**. The small abstract shapes in the landscape depict marked ski slopes, tree clumps and the various activities of the skiers. When looking at the small black, darkly aquatinted shapes, a range of activity is revealed. Even the puffiness of the ski suits becomes apparent. In this way, Doig engages viewers in a visual game, asking them to identify each activity in the cold, snowy environment.

Some of the other works in the *Ten Etchings* series continue the theme of snow-clad landscapes, but also include images of Doig's typical, mysterious views through trees. These tree vistas allow glimpses of buildings with no visible inhabitants, or portray people captured in a quiet, isolated world.

Doig produced this work by etching black outlines on a metal plate and filling in shades of tone using the aquatint technique. In [*no title*], he uses the aquatint technique to create flat, abstract shapes with none of the variation in tone that he uses for instance in *Echo Lake* pictured on page 17. Yet, he manages to compose a mountain scene by carefully placing black, outline shapes onto the white background of the paper. By using a small amount of black, Doig has also managed to conjure the whiteness of the snow, the crisp freshness of the mountain climate and a sense of space – even though this work is on a small scale. Quite magically the slope and activities become alive on the paper.

Aquatint

Aquatint is a method used to produce tonal areas rather than lines. A metal **plate** is covered with grains of rosin, a type of resin, and heated to stick to the surface. The plate is then immersed in a liquid acid solution. The acid eats the metal around the rosin grains and produces small circles that hold ink for printing. Artists can control the darkness of the aquatint by immersing the plate for longer in the acid solution. The area of the aquatint can be controlled by protecting certain parts of the plate from the acid.

My work is about other worlds, geographically and mentally.
PETER DOIG

RICHARD HAMILTON

Richard Hamilton's unique work shows a curiosity for using unusual techniques and methods. He was born in London, UK, in 1922. He studied **draughtsmanship** and worked as a tool designer, and then attended the Slade School of Art. He helped form the 'Independent Group' of artists and writers at the Institute of Contemporary Arts in the 1950s. Here his interest in **Pop Art** developed on the basis that: 'all art is equal whether you are Elvis Presley or Picasso'.

A range of techniques

Hamilton's work as a printmaker combines a range of techniques, which include **engraving**, **etching** and **screenprint**. His images are often digitally altered on the computer and his involvement with print technology has made him one of the leading artists in modern printmaking. He began creating computer-generated works in the 1980s using the software Quantel Desktop Paintbox®. His work is in many public collections throughout the world, including the Scottish National Gallery of Modern Art in Edinburgh, the Fitzwilliam Museum in Cambridge, the British Council, the Tate Gallery in London and the Guggenheim in New York.

Influences

Hamilton lived through the hardships of World War II and then saw a rapid turnabout take place in the USA. Goods that were seen as a luxury before the war, like the vacuum cleaner and fridge, suddenly became affordable to the average person. Hamilton observed this change in popular culture and was influenced by the new images appearing in advertisements. He became one of the leaders of Pop Art in Britain alongside David Hockney (b. 1937) and Eduardo Paolozzi (b. 1924), and was a follower of Marcel Duchamp (see page 7) who used everyday objects in a way that influenced many of the Pop Artists. In 1963 Hamilton visited the USA and came into contact with other Pop Artists like Claes Oldenburg (b. 1929), Robert Rauschenberg (b. 1925) and Andy Warhol (see pages 40–43).

Portrait of Dieter Roth

The subject of this work, Dieter Roth, was a painter, sculptor, collage-maker and printmaker who used everything from chocolate to rabbit droppings to make powerful works of art – he sometimes even drew simultaneously with both hands.

Roth produced a poem and etching called, *My Eye is My Mouth*, based on his idea that the mouth and eye must be fused so that thinking and speaking come from the same source of creativity. In *Portrait of Dieter Roth* (1998), an Iris print made from a digitally altered photograph, Hamilton has captured the energy radiating out of this artist. Ghosting around the face, together with the yellow halo and the brilliant streak of yellow, suggest an aura of light coming out of Roth, while the manipulation of his eyes with their almost laser-beam energy, suggests an unnerving undertone. Using these techniques, Hamilton has produced a portrait which has an energy that both magnetically draws us towards the man, but at the same time disturbs and repels us.

Technique

Dieter Roth's image was taken from a photograph made in the late 1970s for a group exhibition called *Interfaces*. After scanning the photograph into his computer, Hamilton used Quantel Paintbox® to change and blur the image digitally. In a way, the computer became his paintbrush. However he was not happy with the actual printed output. Alongside a number of other ideas, the image lay waiting for computer print technology to catch up and new inks to be produced that would not fade. *Portrait of Dieter Roth* was finally produced in 1998 as an Iris print. An Iris print is a form of printing that was developed in 1987 when the first Iris Inkjet printer was produced. The Iris Inkjet spits out microscopic drops of overlapping cyan, magenta, yellow and black (CMYK) ink through minute, separate nozzles. A typical Iris print is made up of billions of these individual drops of ink. The result is an amazingly rich and intensely coloured print that does not fade. The development of this technology enabled Hamilton finally to achieve the right quality for this work.

Breaking boundaries

In the 1950s, like his fellow artist Paolozzi, Hamilton made collages from advertisements in magazines and newspapers. His famous collage called *Just what is it that makes today's homes so different, so appealing?* was of a room. It was a poster for an exhibition held in London in 1956, which presented images of the post-war era, like the vacuum cleaner, the TV and the comic book. In 1964, Hamilton took a black and white photograph of his original collage and added colour to this by screenprinting Ben Day dots (dots originally used to print colour in comics) on top. He developed this image into a series called *Interior*, which showed variations of the same room. Later in the 1990s, he used a photograph of the same collage again, but this time changed the image digitally. This continual experimentation is typical of Hamilton's style.

> *A **medium** need not sit in isolated purity. It has always been my contention [argument] that the first objective is to achieve a compelling image … As time goes by I become increasingly aware of the irrelevance of making a distinction between one medium and another, or one process and another, or even one style and another.*
> RICHARD HAMILTON

Interior *(1964) is a screenprint of an earlier collage using eight different stencils. It shows various styles of furniture, paintings and pattern as well as a pose of the 'perfect' 1960s woman, in order to reflect the culture of that era.* Interior *was part of a series of screenprints by the same name, all slightly different, and all based on the original collage called* Just what is it that makes today's home so different, so appealing?

By creating images taken from so many sources and combining so many processes, Hamilton uses every available printmaking opportunity to get the most out of the final print. His work shows his originality as a printmaker who is unafraid to test new technology.

WILLIAM KENTRIDGE

William Kentridge is a well-known printmaker, film animator and **draughtsman**. He was born in 1955 in Johannesburg, South Africa, where he continues to live and work. Kentridge studied Politics and African Studies, after which he attended the Johannesburg Art Foundation and from 1981 to 1982 studied Mime and Theatre at the École Jacques Lecoq in Paris. Upon his return to South Africa he worked in the film industry. Kentridge started to draw again in 1985. His first animated film, *Johannesburg, 2nd Greatest City after Paris*, was completed in 1989. Since then Kentridge has established a worldwide reputation for his animated films produced from charcoal drawings. He has participated in major exhibitions in the USA, Europe and China, and the Serpentine Gallery, London, held a survey exhibition for him (an exhibition focusing on a period or aspect of an artist's work) in 1999. Kentridge has recently worked on a series of **intaglio** prints in Johannesburg with the New York master printmaker Randy Hemminghaus (b. 1957).

The artist and the city

Kentridge's artistic output is varied, but he uses the same creative source for all his work – his life and the city of Johannesburg. The artist disliked the dry barrenness of the Johannesburg city landscape until he started drawing it. He saw his drawings of the city almost as a form of revenge against its nothingness. His works are autobiographical and he sees himself and his characters as captives in the city. Kentridge has never been able to escape Johannesburg and he states that his works are 'rooted in this desperate provincial city'.

Brought up in a family of liberal, politically-involved lawyers, the young Kentridge was more aware of the inequalities of the **apartheid** society in which he grew up than most of his age group. The need for change was impressed upon him. When Nelson Mandela, who was imprisoned for his opposition to the system, was set free and apartheid was dismantled, he felt his childhood hopes for a free society came true.

I have never tried to make illustrations of apartheid, but the drawings and films are certainly spawned by and feed off the brutalized society left in its wake. I am interested in a political art, that is to say an art of ambiguity, contradiction, uncompleted gestures, and certain endings; an art (and a politics) in which optimism is kept in check and nihilism [pessimism] at bay. WILLIAM KENTRIDGE

Dreams in film and print

In *Staying Home* (1999), an **etching** from the series *Sleeping on Glass*, there is a connection between animation and print. The film *Sleeping on Glass*, like some of Kentridge's other works, started with a dream. The series incorporates elements of collage as part of the **composition**. Kentridge used old pages from study notes and a structural engineering handbook onto which he printed these intaglio images. The yellowing pages were first neutralised with chemicals to remove excess acid before being laminated on to etching paper. After this, small details and colour were added to the works by hand. In *Staying Home* a row of trees in planters separate the foreground from the trees in the distant background. The nostalgic title *Staying Home* and the trees rooted in soil, contrast with the moveable, potted plants with their artificial, clipped shapes.

Staying Home *(1999), an etching on paper with collage, is based on a drawing Kentridge made in Italy.*

Other influences

Mhlaba Dumile-Feni, an important African sculptor and draughtsman, influenced Kentridge's art. Dumile-Feni made large-scale charcoal drawings that prompted Kentridge to explore the **medium**. Although Kentridge's works are steeped in South African events, he also draws upon European influences. Opera, writers such as Buechner and Goethe, and artists such as George Grosz (1893–1959), Francisco de Goya (1746–1828) and William Hogarth (1697–1764) all play parts in his art making. In fact, Kentridge's drawing style can be compared to early 20th century Berlin **Dadaists** and German **Expressionists**.

General

Although drawing is central to Kentridge's work, he has incorporated and extended it in his animated films and printmaking. *General* (1993–98) is a drypoint etching (where an image is drawn on a **plate** using a sharp needle without the use of acid) printed on hand-painted paper.

General relates to the theatre production *Woyzek on the Highveld* (1992). The story is of a simple soldier who, betrayed by his loved one, stabs her in a fit of jealousy. Kentridge puts this story in a South African context and explores the economic, personal and social pressures that push ordinary people towards violence.

Approach

Kentridge considers this to be a monoprint (where only one print is produced) because the background colour on each sheet is hand painted. It is a 'drypoint' drawn on an acrylic sheet and printed onto paper previously painted in yellow. In the drypoint technique, the burr, or ridge, created by the drawn marks holds an amount of ink which prints as a soft line, especially where lines criss-cross. In *General*, Kentridge uses this blurriness to express the soft flabbiness of the General's facial features. The expressive areas around the eyes, the mouth and the skin folds add to the bleak and sad quality of the portrait. The General's eye staring though the monocle, and the medals on his chest, draw questions from the viewer. Has the General been decorated for being a good soldier, or can only people with restricted vision see war as a solution to conflict? The outward flowing shapes of the sharp yellow paint and the splashed red strokes emphasize the dark atmosphere of this portrait.

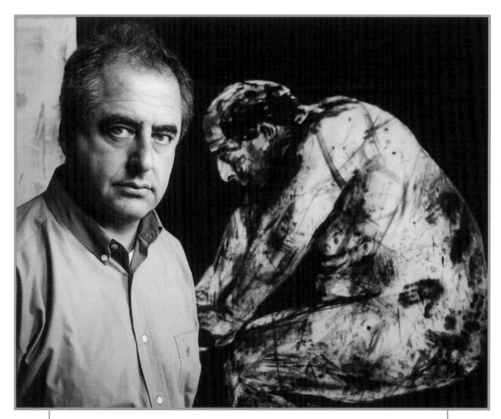

William Kentridge. He often depicts himself in his works.

ROY LICHTENSTEIN

American **Pop Artist**, painter, sculptor and **lithographer**, Roy Lichtenstein, was born in New York City, USA, in 1923. He began drawing as a hobby. After leaving school he studied briefly at the Art Students' League and then went to the School of Fine Art at Ohio State College. His study was interrupted by the outbreak of World War II. He was drafted into the army and served in Britain and Europe. After the war he returned to Ohio State College where he later lectured. In the late 1940s and 1950s he worked in **woodcut**, lithography and **etching** and began experimenting with **screenprint** in the 1960s. He died in 1997 after a long career in printmaking that was experimental and groundbreaking.

A challenge

Lichtenstein's first cartoon image was a result of his son challenging him to paint a comic book Mickey Mouse. He then started to use comic strip imagery in his work making minor changes to the original colour. He also began using images of solitary objects like washing machines, found in newspapers or Yellow Page advertisements. His first one-man show of this type of Pop Art was at the Castelli Gallery in New York. Lichtenstein's work can be seen in galleries and museums throughout the world. His *Times Square Mural* was made of porcelain enamel on steel in 1994, three years before he died. It measures a mammoth 17 metres in length and nearly 2 metres in height and is a gift from the artist to the city of New York.

Influences

Lichtenstein's earliest influences were **Cubism** and **Abstract Expressionism** and the images used by Pablo Picasso. He expanded on work already done by Pop Artists Robert Rauschenberg and Jasper Johns (b. 1930) in the USA and Richard Hamilton and Eduardo Paolozzi in Britain. Along with Andy Warhol, Lichtenstein became part of the Pop Art movement. Pop Art's aim to deal with things that were everyday fitted with his own ideas. He took ordinary objects from the supermarket and the American soda parlour such as the sandwich, the frosted glass with a paper straw wrapper, and the roasted turkey as his themes.

> *It's what people really see. We're not living in a school-of-Paris world, you know, and the things we really see in America are like this. It's McDonald's, it's not Le Corbusier [French architect/designer].*
> ROY LICHTENSTEIN

Lichtenstein's style was two-dimensional with objects and figures often enlarged many times the original size. Mass-produced posters and shopping bags printed with his images added to the idea of his art being easily accessible.

Brush strokes in wood

Although Lichtenstein often combined numerous print processes to produce one image, he sometimes used a single technique to copy another process. In *Vertical Apple,* he used **woodcut** to suggest enormous painted strokes. The design is extraordinarily free and fluid, as if a large paintbrush has been swept across the paper. Although clearly a woodcut, the printed surface manages to have the freshness of a quickly-painted canvas.

Woodcut

Woodcut is a process of **relief printing** made by cutting with a gouge or chisel into the grained surface of a block of wood. The raised portions left behind are inked with a roller and printed. This results in a slightly textured print that is unique to woodcut. It is not as dense as a screenprint. Woodcut is different to wood **engraving** in that in wood engraving, the wood is gouged out on the **end grain** of a block of wood. The grain of the wood in end grain is closer together. As a result the carving can be more detailed and the resulting print is finer.

Comic imagery

Much of Lichtenstein's work was based on the comic book style of using as few lines as possible to show an image. He also made use of dark outlines and enlarged Ben Day dots, which were originally used to show colour in comics. The strong black outlines and shapes are almost **abstract** and force us to look at them closely before we notice the story. Lichtenstein was fascinated not only by the style used in comics but also in the subject of comics – love, heroism and aggression. By using images of aggression in flat comic book style, he could draw on his own wartime experiences and show how easily war and violence is absorbed into popular culture. He often used speech bubbles, sometimes with the sound affects of gunfire, as in the image *CRAK!*, to add to the sharpness of the image.

Reflections on Conversation

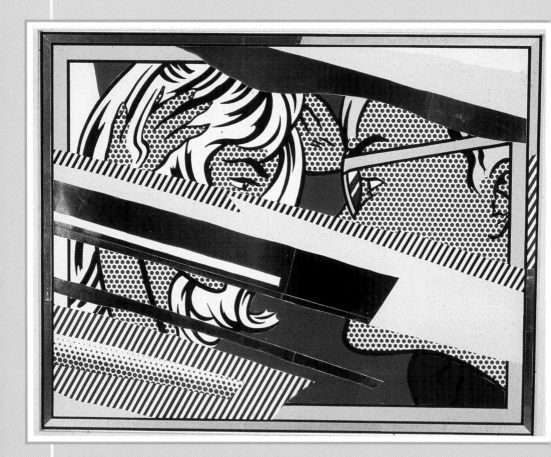

Glass, mirror and reflection were important themes in Lichtenstein's work. *Reflections on Conversation* (1990; screenprint, lithography and woodcut on embossed plastic sheeting) is part of a series printed to look as if the images are behind a reflecting piece of glass.

The girl in *Reflections on Conversation* is one of Lichtenstein's typical willowy blondes who represent the ideal, smiling 'Hollywood' woman. The hero wears glasses and although the couple stare into each other's eyes, the meaning is uncertain. He might be starry-eyed, looking at the world through rose-tinted glasses, even blinded by love, or the glasses could be a barrier to his love. The effect of glass like a screen in front of the viewer is also a barrier. The faces appear fractured. The viewer is prevented from seeing the whole picture. The moment is close up and intimate, but we are only allowed a glimpse into their lives.

The image is a mixture of sweetness and innocence, reminding us of early Hollywood movies, but it also shows tension in the sharp shapes of the reflection across the faces. They could be whispering something extremely innocent or extremely serious. Even the title suggests uncertainty. It is a reflection on what the viewer might overhear.

Technique

Reflections on Conversation with its enlarged Ben Day dots, bright abstract blocks of colour and hard-edged black outlines, is very much in comic strip style. Although a simple image of romance, Lichtenstein has used complex combinations of techniques that include lithography, screenprint, collage, woodcut and fourteen colours, to portray it. Typically, he hides most of the evidence of his working methods, so that it is hard to see which part of the print is screenprinted, where he has used lithography and how he has achieved his colour. The Ben Day dots are overlaid to give different effects. Our eyes do most of the mixing of colour. We 'read' the brown dots against their pale cream background as flesh. Yet on closer inspection the large brown dots are not just brown but in fact flecked with red and black. The soft textures of the woodcut are difficult to see. He has also printed the work onto PVC, a type of stiff plastic sheeting and embossed it (made the surface slightly raised in places) so that the colours catch the light. As a result the shiny effect echoes the idea of glass and reflection.

JULIAN OPIE

Julian Opie depicts the modern world through a wide range of **media** that includes sculpture, vinyl and aluminium cut-outs, billboards, bumper stickers, CD designs and huge **inkjet** wallpaper images.

Born in London, UK, in 1958, Opie studied at Goldsmith's College and held his first solo show at the Lisson Gallery within a year. In 1993 he exhibited at the Hayward Gallery filling both floors with sculpture and his first paintings of *Imagine You Are Driving*. The following year he was commissioned to make his *Perimeter Wall Paintings* for the Wormwood Scrubs Prison in London. He studied further in Italy and France and travelled with solo exhibitions to Hanover, Milan, Geneva and Prague. He has exhibited in the USA as well as in Japan, India and Australia. In 2001 he held a highly successful exhibition at the Lisson Gallery in London where he designed his art catalogue to look like a mail-order brochure. He lives and works in London.

Influences

In the early 1980s, Opie was part of a group known as the 'New British Sculptors'. Subsequently he branched out from sculpture to include other media. He has been associated with artists Damien Hirst (b. 1965), Rachel Whiteread (b. 1963), and Sarah Lucas (b. 1962), all of whom produce highly individual art, but Opie's fresh style is peculiarly his own. He uses the computer to simplify everyday objects, such as cars, traffic lights, buildings, roads, people and even sheep, into pictographs like those used for signposts, or icons in computer games.

> *In computer games, simple graphics create places. A few graves become a graveyard; some castellated walls, a fortress; ten identical trees, a forest. They sit flat and need not be realistic. It is the interactive movement around them and your recognition of a classic type that brings them to life.* JULIAN OPIE

Imagine You Are Driving

Opie was commissioned in 2002 to create a gigantic wallpaper frieze as part of the arts initiative 'Tribe Art', launched by BAR Honda. To create the images, Opie drove the Silverstone track first to experience the feeling of being a racing car driver. Opie designed six huge inkjet printed wallpaper images of the racing drivers in the Honda team. Each image showed a portrait of one of the drivers alongside a view of the track.

Each print measured a vast 40 metres long and 7 metres high – in sharp contrast to the size of the bumper sticker he designed afterwards based on this work. The bumper sticker featured racing driver Jacques Villeneuve, with a central image of the track. Thousands were printed and put into *Time Out* magazine as part of a competition to win tickets to the Grand Prix. From this project came another. Opie produced a series of six Lambda prints (see page 34) based on the original Tribe Art wallpaper images. These were printed in a limited **edition**. *Imagine You Are Driving (fast)/Jacques* (2002), shown here, is part of this series.

Opie shows the track from the driver's or car's viewpoint as if on a computer screen. The simplified, flat image has a dreamlike quality, which draws the viewer into the frame. The viewer experiences a sense of freedom, both exhilarating and unsettling. As the road reels out, you expect to catch up with a competitor. It is like a computer game screen and recreates the hyper-reality of arcade games. Detail is kept to a minimum and conveys just basic information. The portrait is also minimal with its simplified black contour lines and flat solid shapes. The style resembles the way in which Opie produced the portraits of the four members of Blur for their CD, *Blur: The Best Of ...* in 2000.

Opie's approach

Opie first photographs his subjects, then uses Adobe Illustrator® software to edit the images to basic shapes and lines. By reducing the detail he highlights their individuality at the same time – showing the difference in the fall of the hair, the eyebrows, the neckline of a jumper, the body posture. The inkjet images can be printed up to any size and by designing them as wallpaper and bumper stickers, as well as in more limited editions, Opie has made his art more available to all.

Lambda print

A Lambda print is made by exposing heavy-duty photo paper using three laser beams, RGB (red, green and blue), to produce a print with a photographic quality. It is based on the same principle of printing in a traditional photo laboratory, that is exposing paper/film to light, but on a far grander scale. The image can be gigantic. Detail and colour are rich – the black velvety, the colours dense – with none of the drawbacks of inkjet since no actual ink is used. Where an inkjet printer must lay down a series of circular CMYK (cyan, magenta, yellow & black) dots of ink which overlap, a Lambda printer – shown here – blends the red, green and blue together by laser. Each **pixel** is copied at the exact colour and so produces a more exact print.

The virtual world

Opie takes on the virtual world in a playful way. His open-air **installations** juggle scale and space. In *My Aunt's Sheep* and in *Three Shy Animals*, life-size animal outlines on plastic-coated aluminium stand outside in real fields under real trees. Opie's titles in his *Imagine* series – *Imagine It Is Raining, Imagine You Are Driving, Imagine You Are Walking* – are invitations to follow the artist into another reality. We are asked to imagine houses dripping in the rain, the wet landscape passing swiftly, the swish of windscreen wipers, road spray, rain on a roof. Yet Opie's images seem to deny any possibility of rain and discomfort. The houses are neatly arranged. There are no scratches or bumps on his cars. His trees are perfect. It is as if our lives are bombarded with too much detail and Opie is giving us a simplified version.

> *I am always referring to the world, to things that seem poignant [meaningful] to me and then try to synthesize or make my version of these things.* JULIAN OPIE

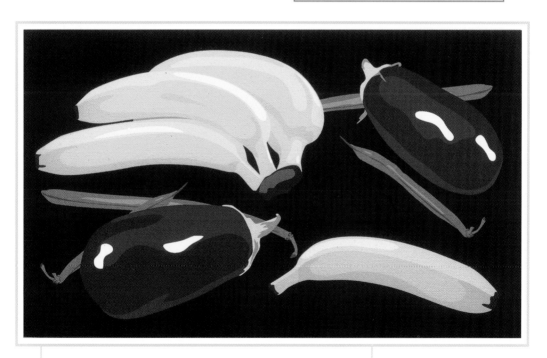

Still Life with Bananas and Aubergine *from* Eight Still Lives *(2001), Lambda print on canvas. This graphic design, with its reduction of detail, is typical of Opie.*

PAULA REGO

Paula Rego is a powerful female voice in the world of printmaking. She was born in Lisbon, Portugal in 1935. She came to London at the age of seventeen to study at the Slade School of Art where she met and married the English painter, Victor Willing. They divided their time between Portugal and England, but eventually settled in England where she lectured at the Slade. Rego's strong **figurative** work is based on a broad range of techniques that includes collage, drawing, painting and **etching**. She became the first Associate Artist at the National Gallery in London, where she painted the huge triptych (three panels) *Crivelli's Garden*, in the Sainsbury Wing Restaurant.

Influences

Rego was brought up on folk tales told by her grandmother and aunt and lived very much in her own imagination. As a child she remembers being excited by a book of etchings of dramatically lit scenes from Dante's *Inferno*, where the poet tells of his journey through the flames of Hell. Rego's own work shows the same element of moody contrast between shadow and brilliant light that is called *chiaroscuro*. The experience of living between the cultures of two countries has had enormous impact on her work. Traditionally in Portugal, men and women led fairly separate lives and the female storyteller spoke on behalf of all women. Rego's figures of women or girls, appear solid, almost peasant-like and linked to the earth. They reflect the people she saw in the Portuguese countryside and show the influence of artists like Jean Dubuffet (1901–1985) and Pablo Picasso.

Hey Diddle Diddle

In her etching of the English nursery rhyme, *Hey Diddle Diddle* (1989), Rego explores a feeling of carnival-like gaiety. Her little girl is skipping. The dog is laughing. The cat is playing the fiddle and the cow floats effortlessly against the starry sky. The moon lights up the scene in a theatrical way and the enormity of the star-strewn sky draws us into the picture. Then the sharp-curved moon directs us back to the girl. We realize she is skipping backwards on the edge of a cliff that drops into space. Suddenly the animals appear different. They appear to be crowding her. The tall muscular cat has a devilish look. We can almost hear the music getting louder and wilder as he edges her backwards. The dog has a knowing grin, the cow looks too smug, and the faceless dish darts for cover under the bushes. What at first seems a game, has turned into something more sinister and dark.

Rego's approach to etching

Rego feels most comfortable with etching as a method of printmaking. Her energetic lines, like those in the cat of *Hey Diddle Diddle*, reflect the direct way she approaches her work. She often draws on the copper **plate** without sketching first. This method echoes the way in which a child will pick up a crayon and begin to draw. If a line needs to be changed she will paste over it and draw it again.

> Drawing is essential to all Rego's work. Her advice to students is: *Just keep drawing. And keep a few secrets for yourself. Don't show everything to everybody … particularly the teachers. Keep it secret.* PAULA REGO

After drawing on the plate, Rego works with artist Paul Coldwell, who helps plan how deep the line should be etched and how dark it should be when printed.

Etching is a process where a metal plate (copper, steel or zinc) is covered with an acid resistant 'ground'. The artist draws through the ground but not into the metal, with a sharp tool. The plate is then put into acid. The acid bites into it where the metal has been exposed but not into the area covered by ground. The ground is then removed, the plate rolled with ink, and then wiped clean. Ink left behind in the etched lines on the plate, is printed on to the paper when the plate is put through a press. The longer the plate is exposed to the acid, the deeper the bite and therefore the stronger or darker the line.

The next stage is to add layers of tone. This process is called aquatint (see page 19). Parts that remain white, like the moon and area of the cow in *Hey Diddle Diddle* are blocked or 'stopped out' with wax or varnish, then the plate has rosin heated on to it to create texture. The longer the plate is dipped in acid the deeper the texture and therefore the darker the tone.

Stories without text

In her twelve etchings of *The Pendle Witches*, Rego illustrates a poem by the English poet Blake Morrison (b. 1950) about the witches who were put on trial in the town of Pendle, Lancaster, in the UK during the rule of King James I. *The Flood*, which comes from this series, shows a heavy-limbed woman crammed uncomfortably in a tub. The woman's awkwardness is shared by the viewer. This feeling of discomfort often features in Rego's work. We sense a feeling of doom. The tones of the aquatint highlight the swirling water, the stormy sky and the sharp streaks of rain. The woman makes no effort to protect herself except for a half-hearted hand over her head. Her state of undress makes her appear even more exposed to danger. There is a dreamlike quality to the chaos and strange creatures floating around her. Is this Noah's Flood? Does it suggest woman's ability to survive? Her inner strength? Or perhaps her helplessness?

The Flood *(1996), an etching from the series,* The Pendle Witches.

In her etchings, Rego allows the viewer a glimpse into scenes that appear ordinary, yet a sense of danger lurks below the surface. There is a nightmarish quality that is sinister, looming and catastrophic.

ANDY WARHOL

Andy Warhol has been considered a genius of his time. Born in Pittsburgh, Pennsylvania, USA, in 1928, Warhol's parents were Czechoslovakian immigrants. He attended the Carnegie Institute of Technology in Pittsburgh studying Design, and then moved immediately to New York and began his career as a commercial artist.

In the 1960s, Warhol produced the **screenprint** images for which he became most well known. They range from Coca Cola® bottles, Campbell Soup cans and dollar bills, to famous people like Marilyn Monroe. Based on popular culture, they reflect his fascination with images of mass consumption. His work is exhibited in galleries and museums throughout the world. The Andy Warhol Museum opened in Pittsburgh, USA, in 1994.

Pop Art and The Factory

After World War II the American way of life changed. It was the era of the vacuum cleaner, the TV, the washing machine and many other items that made life easier. The supermarket replaced the corner store. Warhol used images of everyday products like Coke® bottles and beer cans as symbols of this society. He repeated them over and over to highlight the idea of mass production and availability.

Connecting with his theme of mass production, he called his studio 'The Factory'. It was an industrial loft space in midtown Manhattan, New York City, where his screenprints, paintings, photographs and later his films, videos and *Interview* magazine, were produced. A constant stream of art dealers, celebrities, fashion designers and pop stars came and went and it became the artistic hotspot in New York.

> *You can be watching TV and see Coca-Cola, and you know that the President drinks Coke, Liz Taylor drinks Coke, and just think, you can drink Coke too. A Coke is a Coke and no amount of money can get you a better Coke than the one the bum on the corner is drinking.* ANDY WARHOL

Superman *(1981). Screenprint on paper. Warhol loved to use images from popular culture and the* Superman *films were hugely popular in the 1970s and 1980s.*

Diamond dust, disasters and shadows

In his screenprint series *Myths*, Warhol used childhood heroes and fantasy figures and added a layer of diamond dust to reflect a child's fascination with glitter. His *Disaster* series shows brutal images inspired by press photographs. He used the image of *The Electric Chair* repeatedly as the morality of the death penalty was debated. A photograph of a shadow in his studio inspired his later screenprint series, *Shadows*. The idea of shadow is hard to grasp. It is an image of nothing and yet also something in its own right. Warhol's *Shadows* are very real. Perhaps they are the trace of his thoughts on death. He died unexpectedly after an operation in 1987 at the age of 65.

Marilyn

Warhol's images of film star Marilyn Monroe, actress Liz Taylor, president's wife Jackie Kennedy and singer Elvis Presley, express the American obsession with fame and reflect the superficiality of modern society. Warhol made the work below, *Marilyn, right hand side* in 1964.

Famous people became icons or symbols. Everything they did was written about, and their lives were made public. They were like 'products' on a supermarket shelf. Marilyn Monroe was a famous actress who was supposedly the typical beautiful blonde woman of all men's dreams. She became known as a 'pin-up' – a girl whose photograph men in the 1950s pinned up in the workplace or in their homes. After her death, Warhol made more than 20 screenprints of her, based on a photograph from the 1953 film, *Niagara*. By repeating the image again and again – known as multiples – he highlights the wide distribution of her image throughout the **mass media** of TV, film and print. She was a 'product'. In doing so he perhaps reflects what drove Monroe to end her life by taking an overdose of sleeping pills.

Focusing in on the image

By cutting the photographic image to show only Marilyn's face and emphasizing her lips, eyes and hair, Warhol created not so much a likeness but a symbol of the perfect 'pin-up'. The image focuses on the features that represented Marilyn Monroe in the public imagination: the blonde-dyed hair, the wide smile, the full lips, the sultry long-lashed eyes.

Using screenprinting effects

By using screenprint, Warhol deliberately chose a printing technique associated with commercial advertising. This accentuated the fact that Marilyn's face was a commodity or product. The images are super-charged with colour – the backgrounds bright, the eye shadow brilliant. The red of her face jumps out with such intensity that by comparison the grey or green shadows in her hair and below her cheekbones, look pale instead of dark. This gives the image the appearance of a negative where dark and light is reversed. It has a ghostlike effect. The viewer wonders if the person might disappear or fade away completely.

Warhol has purposefully overlapped, or misaligned, the different layers of stencils while screenprinting, so colours are not printed within the outline. This gives a sense of vibration around the face, which might suggest the shimmer of 'stardom' but emphasizes the idea of her not being real. The images ask the question: Do we know the real Marilyn?

Screenprint

Screenprinting is a stencil printing technique. A screen is stretched over a frame and parts are blocked out with a stencil. Ink is then dragged across the screen with a rubber squeegee. The ink passes through the areas that are not blocked off and prints onto the paper underneath. Several screens are used to achieve different colours. In modern screenprinting, photographic techniques are often used to create negative stencils from which positive images can be printed.

KIM WESTCOTT

The artist Kim Westcott is a master printmaker and painter. Westcott was born in 1968 in Melbourne, Australia. She graduated from the Victoria College of the Arts in 1989 and afterwards joined the Australian Print Workshop as an assistant. Westcott took a break from the Workshop to travel to Dimboola and the Little Desert region of Victoria in 1992. Garner Tullis, the American printmaker, invited Westcott to New York and in 1994 she worked as a master printer in his workshop. Westcott's desire to continue her work on the Australian landscape prompted her return home where she travelled to Utopia and worked with the acclaimed Aboriginal artist, Emily Kame Kngwarreye. After a spell in Mornington Peninsula, Westcott settled in West Brunswick, Melbourne, where she set up her own studio. Westcott's most recent European exhibition was at the t'Ulenest Sculpture Park in the Netherlands.

Rhythms in nature, language and music

The most important influences on Westcott's work are her personal life experiences and travels in the Australian bush. The trip to Dimboola was the first opportunity she had to work directly from the environment. The experience made her more aware of the qualities of space, colour, texture and pattern in the Australian landscape. Westcott not only uses the landscape as an inspiration, but also refers to rhythmic patterns from music and language.

Since leaving art school, Westcott has concentrated on drypoint techniques (see pages 26–27) and developed a unique visual language of her own. Her works can be seen as being both **abstract** and representational. Westcott's earlier drypoint **etchings** displayed a tight grid-like structure that has gradually softened to take on a more **organic** and irregular quality. It is possible that the Australian landscape softened the impact that New York and the influence of modernist artists such as Robert Ryman (b. 1930) had upon her work.

Kim Westcott (right) and her assistant Jo Darvell (left) in her studio in West Brunswick, Victoria, Australia.

Alad Bird

The references to natural forms in a work such as *Alad Bird* (1996; dry point on paper) are obvious, but they can also easily be seen as abstract forms. The curious linear shapes that Westcott creates are from natural objects such as weather beaten branches. In *Alad Bird* the artist has created a print using a range of drypoint marks ranging from light, delicate trails to dark, expressive lines and dots. Following the movement of the lines and dots, different landscapes and views appear in the picture through twisted branches.

> *... the tea-trees and she-oaks are affected by the harsh climatic conditions of the coastal environment, so you have these wild eccentric, twisted tree forms. I saw the branches as lines and the leaves as dots ...* KIM WESTCOTT

Technique

Since 1995 Westcott has brought a new dimension to printmaking by her process of drypoint **encaustic** painting in which she combines printmaking with painting techniques. In her latest work the artist's imagery seems earthier and resembles aspects of Aboriginal art.

ADRIAN WISZNIEWSKI

Painter, **draughtsman** and printmaker, Adrian Wiszniewski was born in 1958 in Glasgow, Scotland. He studied at the Mackintosh School of Architecture and the Glasgow School of Art. He held his first solo exhibition in Glasgow and London in 1984. His printmaking techniques cover **etching**, **screenprint**, **woodcut**, **linocut** and **lithography** but his openness to experimentation has led him to ceramics, TV screenplays, flag and even carpet design. He constantly seeks projects that test and expand the way he works. He has also exhibited in Belgium, Japan and Australia and his work is in the Museum of Modern Art in New York, the Scottish National Gallery of Modern Art in Edinburgh, the Tate Gallery and the Victoria and Albert Museum in London.

Growing up in Glasgow

Adrian Wiszniewski became one of the young 'New Glasgow Boys' in the 1980s. The group included fellow Glasgow artists, Steven Campbell (b. 1953), Ken Currie (b. 1960) and Peter Howson (b. 1958). They were influenced by the German painters, Georg Baselitz (b. 1938), A. R. Penck (b. 1939), and Jörg Immendorf (b. 1945), who were known as the 'New Wild Ones' and produced large-scale sometimes violent **figurative** works. **Neo-Expressionism** is the term given to this type of art where reality is changed or distorted by the artist's own emotions.

In the 1980s Glasgow had a reputation for unemployment and a violent gang culture. The work of the New Glasgow Boys was based on the theme of 'man as a hero', in the face of this social and urban unrest. They painted in a style that was almost cartoon-like where shapes were often distorted and colours were strong. Their work has been called 'New Image'.

The influence of Henri Matisse is also strong in Wiszniewski's work. His series of 12 banners, entitled *Newleafland Flags*, painted in flat solid shapes of colour, is a tribute to the 20 stencilled images in Matisse's work, *Jazz*. This tribute is also evident in Wiszniewski's screenprint, *Interior with Violence*, based on Matisse's painting, *Interior with Violin*, as well as in his screenprint/lithograph, *Bather Four*, based on Matisse's sculpture of the same name. Wiszniewski's first linocuts were a series entitled, *For Max*, named after his son who was born in 1987.

Men in conversation

Wiszniewski's work is full of questions. It often portrays the male figure in surroundings and demands a response from the viewer. He describes his art as a conversation between the figure and his world.

His poetic-looking men have wide eyes and elongated bodies. Placed in settings which are almost dreamlike, there is a mixture of fact and witty fantasy that fools and intrigues the eye. In the woodcut, *Kunst,* which means art in German, a sculptor seems to discover his face in the wood he is carving which is Wiesniewski's playful way of suggesting he found his own self in his woodcut.

Trying to Make a Dollar shows a man in a small room with what at first appears to be a snake and another man fending it off with a pole. The snake and pole are in fact pieces of a dollar sign being made. The image seems to suggest that making a dollar is a difficult process. Wiszniewski not only plays with words and image, but also with technique. The expanse of solid colour, the sharp outlines and black textures, makes it seem as though this piece is a linocut, whereas it is in fact a screenprint, with the final black-inked screen overlaid at the end. Once again Wiszniewski has fooled and intrigued the eye.

Trying to Make a Dollar *(1991), screenprint on paper. Both men wear working clothes and are barefoot, which make them seem unprotected.*

A man noticed a box. *Image 1, from the series* For Max *(1988).*

For Max

For Max (1988; linocut on paper) was the result of a publisher, Charles Booth-Clibborn of Paragon Press, sending Wiszniewski a batch of lino blocks to make into an artist's book. The story tells of a man who finds a strange object in a box and sets out to discover what its use is. It has no printed text but is told entirely with pictures. Wiszniewski playfully invites the viewer to add his own storyline. A few years after completing the series he finally wrote the words of the story in a single copy of the book.

Technique

The linocuts were made without preliminary (initial) sketches. Wiszniewski drew directly on to the lino blocks with a black felt-tipped marker pen, making up the story as he went along. He completed the drawings in one afternoon and spent the next few days cutting the 25 images. Like the lines of his drawings, the grooves of his cuts appear as a single fluid motion. This gives a sense of freshness to the work. Each image is printed in a single colour. He has given the book poetic rhythm by dividing it into 3 groups of 7 colours and 1 group of 4 colours. The 7th, 14th and 21st images are printed in black to mark these divisions.

The fishing-friend uprooted the object but it was a plant! *Image 7 from the series,* For Max *(1988).*

Linocut

In linocut the artist uses a gouge (knife) to cut into a piece of linoleum (a material made up of cork mixed with linseed oil on a canvas base usually used as floor covering) to make the design. Different blades achieve different marks that can be wide or fine depending on the shape of the blade and depending how deeply the line is cut. The cut can be made to produce a single line or smaller marks made to produce texture. The lino block is then inked and printed either by passing the paper and the lino through a press or printing manually on to paper. Large areas of lino left uncut will produce large flat areas of colour. A linocut can either be in a single colour or more colours can be added by overprinting with further blocks.

The situation in my pictures is never resolved … I'd rather paint questions than answers. That way you are not preaching you're discussing things with the viewer. ADRIAN WISZNIEWSKI

TIMELINE

Prehistory	**Engraving** first used in cave art on rocks and bones
400s	The **woodcut** is used in China to print textiles
1151	First European paper is produced in Játava, Spain
Late 1300s	The woodcut is used in Europe for textile printing
1446	Earliest dated print engraving is produced in Germany
1513	First dated **etching** is made by Swiss artist Urs Graf
Early 1600s	**Mezzotint** is developed by Ludwig von Siegen
1600s	*Ukiyo-e* school of printmaking emerges in Japan
Late 1700s	Thomas Bewick develops wood engraving technique in England
1769	Royal Academy of Art in London is founded
1798	Alois Senefelder discovers **lithography** process in Munich
1839	Frenchman Louis Daguerre (1789–1851) produces first commercially successful photographs – the daguerreotype
1879	Ben Day dots invented by Benjamin Day
1881	Pablo Picasso is born in Málaga, Spain. He is responsible for the revival of the print in the 20th century.
1912	**Cubists** begin to experiment with collage technique
1914–18	World War I
1917	Marcel Duchamp, the French **Dadaist**, exhibits 'readymades', including *Fountain*, a porcelain urinal
1922	Richard Hamilton is born in London, UK
1923	Roy Lichtenstein is born in New York, USA
1928	Andy Warhol is born in Pittsburg, USA
1929	MoMA, the first major American museum devoted to 20th century art is founded in New York.
	Stock market crashes causing the Great Depression
1934	Comic strip artist Alex Raymond creates *Flash Gordon*. Eleven-year-old Roy Lichtenstein becomes an avid fan.
	Paula Rego is born in Lisbon, Portugal
1938	Vija Celmins is born in Riga, Latvia
1939	World War II breaks out
1948	**Abstract Expressionism** starts to develop
*c.*1950	Picasso and Matisse adopt and popularise **linocut** process
1953	Elvis Presley makes his first record
1955	William Kentridge is born in Johannesburg, South Africa
1956	Richard Hamilton's collage poster, *Just what is it that makes today's homes so different, so appealing?* marks beginning of **Pop Art** movement

1957	Chila Kumari Burman is born in Liverpool, England
1958	Julian Opie is born in London, England
	Adrian Wiszniewski is born in Glasgow, Scotland
1959	Peter Doig is born in Edinburgh, Scotland
1960	Warhol starts making hand-painted pictures based on comic strips and advertisements
1961	Roy Lichtenstein paints Mickey Mouse and other comic images
1962	Warhol produces **screenprints** of Marilyn Monroe after her death. The first important exhibition of Pop Art, *The New Realists*, takes place in New York.
1967	Warhol produces the first album cover for the band *Velvet Underground*
1968	Kim Westcott is born in Melbourne, Australia
1969	Woodstock Art and Music Festival and Neil Armstrong's walk on the Moon becomes a source of inspiration for artists like Warhol and Celmins
1980	CDs appear in shops and the age of digital image manipulation begins
1983	Julian Opie's first solo show at the Lisson Gallery, London
	Peter Doig's first solo exhibition in America
1987	Warhol dies unexpectedly after an operation
1988	Adrian Wiszniewski produces *For Max* linocuts. The World Wide Web (www) is developed in Switzerland.
1992	Richard Hamilton produces computer-generated updated version of the 1956 collage *Just what is it that makes today's homes so different?* – 150,000 British radio listeners enter competition for 5000 prints
1997	Roy Lichtenstein dies
2000	Julian Opie designs CD cover, *Blur: the best of ...*
	Tate Modern opens on Bankside, London, exhibiting prints alongside major paintings
2001	Peter Doig publishes *100 Years Ago 2001*, a series of eight colour etchings with The Paragon Press
2002	*Imagine You Are Driving (fast)* series of Lambda prints by Julian Opie exhibited for the first time at the Alan Cristea Gallery, London
2003	New Saatchi Gallery opens in County Hall, South Bank, London.

GLOSSARY

abstract art that does not imitate or represent physical reality, sometimes referred to as non-figurative or non-representational

Abstract Expressionism style of art that emerged in New York in the 1940s, often showing freely scribbled marks as in Jackson Pollock's work

apartheid separating people based on race or colour. A policy adopted by the South African Nationalist Government in 1948.

Cibachrome high quality photographic printing process on to plastic paper. Also known as a C-Print.

composition arrangement of elements or objects in an artwork

conceptual artwork where the idea is considered more important than the actual end product

Cubism art movement led by Picasso and Braque and begun in around 1907, in which three-dimensional facets or sides of a single object are shown on a flat surface

Dadaists group of artists who started an art movement in Zürich in 1916. They wanted to free themselves from all artistic conventions.

digital printing laser or inkjet printing where the signal to output comes from a computer

draughtsman someone who is good at the technical aspects of drawing

edition complete number of prints 'pulled' (pulled away) from the plate, stone, block or screen and numbered and signed by the artist

encaustic hot wax painting technique that combines beeswax, resin and pigments. Heat is used to blend the paint mixture and then to apply the paint on to a canvas support.

end grain woodblock cut across the grain of a tree trunk. End grain is suitable for fine detail.

engraving process of cutting into metal plates or wood with a burin. A burin is a square-shaped steel rod sliced through at a slant to make a diamond-shaped head that has a sharp point and produces a clean-edged line.

etching intaglio printing process where metal plates are covered with acid-resistant layers. A sharp tool is used to draw a design onto the plate, which is then etched in an acid solution.

Expressionism/Expressionist art movement begun in France but most popular in Germany in the early 1900s. It often showed exaggerated and distorted forms and colours. Expressionists include Wassily Kandinsky and Paul Klee.

figurative art that represents reality where recognizable figures and objects are portrayed

inkjet printing directly to paper or material from a digital file by means of a stream of fine quick-drying ink drops, controlled by the computer

installation particular way in which the artist or curator arranges artworks in an exhibition space which relies on the space as part of the effect

intaglio from the Italian word meaning 'to cut into'. It refers to printmaking processes that include etching, engraving, aquatint and mezzotint. Ink is pressed into lines cut into the surface of the plate. The pressure of the printing press enables the ink to be lifted and transferred on to paper.

introspection looking inward and thinking about your own emotional state

kitsch sentimental art which is often garish and attempts to be cute

laser print a print produced on a printer, which uses toner rather than ink to produce images through a combination of heat and laser beams

linocut relief method of printing using linoleum blocks cut with a gouge

lithography method in which the stone or plate from which the print is taken, is completely flat. The method is based upon the principle that grease repels water. An image is made in a greasy medium. The surface is then dampened with water and oily ink applied with a roller, and sticks only to the drawing.

mass media media like television, newspapers, magazines and radio that communicate with large sectors of the public

medium/media different types of material, such as paint, ink; also different types of art form, like painting, collage, printmaking

mezzotint intaglio process where the plate is roughened to make ridges and then the design is polished to make the plate smooth in places to produce a range of tones that form an image

Neo-Expressionism violent figurative (non-abstract) art where reality is distorted in the shapes as well as in the use of colour

organic natural design, development or growth as in plants or human organs

photogravure process in which a photographic image is transferred on to an etching plate

pixel minute dots that make up a solid area of colour and brightness on a digital screen. In magnified form the pixels appear as blocks.

plate copper, steel or zinc metallic plate used in intaglio printing

Pop Art movement started in the USA in the 1950s with images that were based on popular culture, such as Coke bottles

Post-Impressionism art movement after Impressionism. The main exponents were Paul Cézanne, Paul Gauguin and Vincent van Gogh. These artists explored colour, line and composition in new ways.

print-run collective result of running an image through a press at a single session

relief print print taken from the raised inked surface of a linoleum block or woodcut

screenprint method of stencil printmaking in which ink is pulled through a meshed surface stretched across a frame

still life print or painting of an immovable object, for example fruit

Surrealism type of art begun in the 1920s that was inspired by dreams and fantasies

woodcut relief print carved on the plank side of a block of wood

WHAT PAPER IS SUITABLE FOR PRINTMAKING?

Printmaking papers are usually 100 per cent rag papers made from cotton or cotton and linen mixtures. The papers are acid free so that they resist ageing. Digital fine art papers have recently been developed that retain quality over time similar to traditional papers. These digital papers must however be used in conjunction with special inks that are lightfast (do not deteriorate in the light). If used correctly, digital inks and papers should ensure a light fastness of 100–200 years.

There are many printmaking papers available from established paper manufacturers in Great Britain, France, Italy and Germany for both conventional and digital printmaking. There are also papers available from Japan and Thailand. These include mulberry papers made from *kozo*, a long rough fibre obtained from mulberry trees, and various decorated papers suited to relief printing.

FURTHER READING

These books are for advanced students but they will be useful for studying particular prints or artists:

Vija Celmins, M.E. Feldman, *Art Monthly*, 202, Dec1996/Jan1997: 32–3.

Contemporary British Art in Print, P. Elliot & C. Booth Clibborn (Edinburgh: Scottish National Gallery of Modern Art, 1995).

The Contemporary Print: from Pre-Pop to Postmodern, S. Tallman (London: Thames & Hudson, 1996).

Peter Doig: a Hunter in the Snow, P. Bonaventura, *Artefactum*, 11(53) Autumn 1994: 12–15.

Great Prints of the 20th Century: Picasso to Hockney, P. Gilmour (Aylesbury: Buckinghamshire County Museum, 1999).

William Kentridge, C. Christov-Bakargiev (Brussels: Sociétè des Expositions du Palais des Beaux-Arts de Bruxelles, 1998).

Pop Impressions Europe/USA: Prints and Multiples from the Museum of Modern Art, W. Weitman (New York: MoMA, 1999).

Paula Rego, F. Bradley (London: Tate Publishing, 2002).

WHERE TO SEE WORKS

You can see prints by the artists in this book as well as other well-known printmakers at the following museums and galleries:

MUSEUMS AND GALLERIES
Ashmolean Museum, Oxford, UK. www.ashmol.ox.ac.uk
British Library, London, UK. www.bl.uk
British Museum, London, UK. www.thebritishmuseum.ac.uk
The Scottish National Gallery of Modern Art, Edinburgh, Scotland.
     www.nationalgalleries.org
Tate Britain, Modern, London, Liverpool & St Ives, UK. www.tate.org.uk
Victoria & Albert Museum, London, UK. www.vam.ac.uk
Art Gallery of New South Wales, Sydney, Australia. www.artgallery.nsw.gov.au
National Gallery of Australia, Canberra, Australia. www.australiaprints.gov.au

SMALLER GALLERIES
Alan Cristea Gallery, London www.alancristea.com
Lisson Gallery, London www.lissongallery.com
Marlborough Fine Art, London www.marlboroughfineart.com

WEB SITES AND LINKS

Explore these exciting web sites to see more prints made by Vija Celmins, Peter Doig, Julian Opie, Paula Rego and Adrian Wiszniewski and many other important artists:

www.advancedgraphics.co.uk – Advanced Graphics London
www.warholfoundation.org – Andy Warhol Foundation
www.australianprintworkshop.com – Australian Print Workshop
www.thecurwenstudio.co.uk – The Curwen Studio
www.edinburgh-printmakers.co.uk – Edinburgh Printmakers Workshop
www.garnertullis.com – Garner Tullis
www.nga.gov/gemini – Gemini G.E.L.
www.gpsart.co.uk – Glasgow Print Studio
www.lichtensteinfoundation.org – Lichtenstein and Beyond
www.paragonpress.co.uk – Paragon Press
www.unm.edu/~tamarind – The Tamarind Institute
www.thinkquest.org/library – ThinkQuest Internet Library
www.moma.org/whatisaprint/flash.html – What is a print?
www.wilhelm-research.com – Wilhelm Imaging Research, Inc.

INDEX